DINOSAUR MADNESS

Absurd Jokes From Prehistoric Times
For Kids Ages 7-11

by Joel Rothman

Published by:
Humor House, Inc.
Flat 1
12 Ornan Road
Belsize Park
London, NW3 4PX
England

Phone: (44) 207-431-0873
Email: joelrothman@btconnect.com

ISBN: 978-1-930596-55-3

Distributed by:
The Guest Cottage, Inc
8821 Hwy 47
P.O. Box 848
Woodruff, WI 54568

Phone: 800-333-8122
        715-358-5195
Fax: 715-358-9456
Email: nancytheguestcottage.com

What did the female dinosaur say when she laid a square egg?
OUCH!

What does a mother dinosaur need when her baby hatches?
Great big diapers!

When the female dinosaur saw one of her eggs hatch with a two-headed baby she said, "They'll be the smartest dinosaurs in the whole world —— after all, two heads are better than one."

I JUST ATE
TEN FROGS —
WILL I LIVE?
IT'S FOR SURE YOU'RE
GONNA CROAK!
ACHE!

What did the young dinosaur say after eating three pounds of strawberries covered with five pounds of horse manure?
"Delicious!"

What's prehistoric, enormous and smelly?
A Brontosaurus's behind!

"Do dinosaurs stink?"
"No —— they're ex-stinct."

What should you do if a Brontosaurus breaks wind?
Get a gas mask —— fast!

11

Why is the head of Tyrannosaurus Rex so far from his toes?
Because his feet smell terrible!

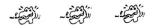

What did the Brontosaurus say to the skunk?
"I really like the deodorant you use!"

A Stegosaurus strolled into the chemist shop and said, "I'd like something to take away my smell." "So would I," said the chemist, "So would I."

The Stegosaurus went to a doctor and complained, "All my friends say I have B.O." The doctor replied, "And what makes you think they are right you disgustingly foul and smelly beast?"

Baryonyx, the super clawed dinosaur, played the part of Saint Nick at Christmas. He was known as *Santa Claws!*

Brontosaurus: How did you cure your son from biting his claws?
Baryonyx: I knocked out all his teeth!

What did the dinosaur's mother warn her children not to do?
"Don't play with children who pick their nose —— they're snotty kids!"

How do you cut a Brontosaurus in two?
With a dino-saw!

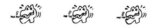

Cross an owl with a dinosaur and what do you get?
An enormous bird that frightens people, but doesn't give a hoot!

What do you get by crossing a dinosaur with a cat?
A neighborhood without dogs!

HE'S MUCH BETTER THAN A WATCHDOG — SINCE WE GOT HIM THERE'S BEEN NO PROBLEM WITH INTRUDERS!

Son: Can you tell me about prehistoric times?

Father: Not really.

Son: Were there people living on Earth 65 million years ago?

Father: I don't know.

Son: Do you know anything about dinosaurs?

Father: No.

Son: Didn't you ever read anything about dinosaurs?

Father: No.

Son: Do you mind me asking questions?

Father: Of course not. You'll never learn anything unless you ask questions.

Female dinosaur: What's your new boyfriend like?

Friend: He's mean, nasty, dirty, smelly, selfish —— and those are just his good points!

Tyrannosaurus Rex phoned a human girl to go out on a blind date. The girl accepted and said, "I'll meet you at the bus stop, but how will I recognize you?"

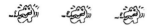

I DO LOVE YOU —
I JUST DON'T THINK
MY PARENTS WILL
APPROVE!

Tyrannosaurus Rex was such a kind-hearted dinosaur —— when he saw a baby bird in a nest without its mother he went and sat on it to keep it warm!

AS A YOUNG DINOSAUR YOU'RE
KIND, GENTLE, LOVEABLE AND
CONSIDERATE. IN SHORT, YOU'RE
A COMPLETE AND UTTER FAILURE!

How do you know if a dinosaur is hiding under your bed?
You'll wake up with your nose squashed against the ceiling!

WHAT DO YOU GET IF YOU CROSS A DINOSAUR WITH A ROSE?
I'M NOT SURE, BUT I WOULDN'T TRY SMELLING IT!

How do you know when a dinosaur has been to College?
From the great big 'C' on his sweater.

Why did the teenage dinosaur need a big axe?
To burst his pimples!

What should you give a seasick dinosaur?
An awful lot of room!

How do you cut a Brontosaurus in two?
With a dino-saw!

Cross an owl with a dinosaur and what do you get?
An enormous bird that frightens people, but doesn't give a hoot!

What do you get by crossing a dinosaur with a cat?
A neighborhood without dogs!

HE'S MUCH BETTER THAN A WATCHDOG — SINCE WE GOT HIM THERE'S BEEN NO PROBLEM WITH INTRUDERS!

Son: Can you tell me about prehistoric times?

Father: Not really.

Son: Were there people living on Earth 65 million years ago?

Father: I don't know.

Son: Do you know anything about dinosaurs?

Father: No.

Son: Didn't you ever read anything about dinosaurs?

Father: No.

Son: Do you mind me asking questions?

Father: Of course not. You'll never learn anything unless you ask questions.

Female dinosaur: **What's your new boyfriend like?**
Friend: **He's mean, nasty, dirty, smelly, selfish —— and those are just his good points!**

I DO LIKE MY MEN TO BE TALL, DARK AND UGLY!

Tyrannosaurus Rex phoned a human girl to go out on a blind date. The girl accepted and said, "I'll meet you at the bus stop, but how will I recognize you?"

I DO LOVE YOU ——
I JUST DON'T THINK
MY PARENTS WILL
APPROVE!

Tyrannosaurus Rex was such a kind-hearted dinosaur —— when he saw a baby bird in a nest without its mother he went and sat on it to keep it warm!

How do you know if a dinosaur is hiding under your bed?
You'll wake up with your nose squashed against the ceiling!

WHAT DO YOU GET IF YOU CROSS A DINOSAUR WITH A ROSE?
I'M NOT SURE, BUT I WOULDN'T TRY SMELLING IT!

How do you know when a dinosaur has been to College?
From the great big 'C' on his sweater.

Why did the teenage dinosaur need a big axe?
To burst his pimples!

What should you give a seasick dinosaur?
An awful lot of room!

What do you get if you cross a parrot with a Stegosaurus?
A lot of big talk!

Cross a rooster with a Megalosaurus and what do you get?
The biggest cluck in town!

What do you get if you cross a porcupine with a Brontosaurus?
A dinosaur who looks like he's undergoing acupuncture!

If you cross a monkey with a dinosaur you wind up with a giant reptile who keeps snapping branches as it swings through the trees.

I don't want to say that the wife of Tyrannosaurus Rex was ugly, but she went to the beauty parlor on Monday and didn't come out till Friday!

How do you know the restaurant where Tyrannosaurus Rex eats has good food?
One million flies can't be wrong!

How do you know when a dinosaur is about to charge?
It takes out its American Express Card.

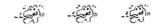

What do you call a bad dream in which you're being chased by a dinosaur?
A bitemare!

DAD —— I THINK YOU SHOULD ROLL UP YOUR WINDOW!

Roman: I've just got a new pet dinosaur. Would you like to take him for his first walk?
Zackary: Is he dangerous?
Roman: I'm not sure —— that's what I want to find out.

What's worse than being mugged by a Brontosaurus?
Being hugged by a Brontosaurus!

What did the Iquanodon say to his victims?
"It's been nice gnawing you!"

Cross a dinosaur with a mouse and you wind up with a truly Mighty Mouse.

You also get great big holes in your wall.

HONEY —— I THINK WE HAVE A PROBLEM!

Tyrannosaurus Rex walked into an ice cream parlor and said, "I'll take the usual."

The man behind the fountain looked at Rex and said, "I serve over 100 people each day. Do you really expect me to remember what *you* order?"

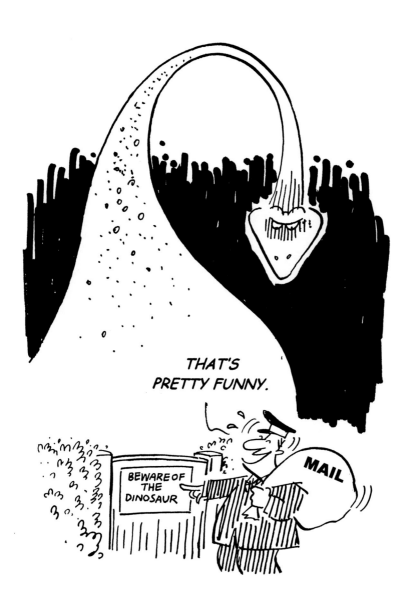

What dinosuar does a cowboy ride in a rodeo?
A bucking bronco-saurus.

Cross a dinosaur with a centipede and what do you get?
A dinosaur with lovely legs, legs, legs, legs, legs, legs . . .

What do you get if you cross a dinosaur with a computer?
A prehistoric know-it-all.

Name the famous dinosaur detective.
Sherlock Rex.

A small boy was looking at the skeleton of a huge dinosaur in the museum and asked, "Why does it have such a long neck?"
His father answered, "The dinosaur's head was so far from his body that a long neck was absolutely necessary!"

The long-necked dinosaur had to eat a meal in the early morning if it wanted the food in its stomach by noon.